praise **J. W**

"[R]aw, and smart, and funny, and sexy, and all the things I love in a poet, wrapped up in one package. Read this book, STAT!"

—*Heather, Five-Star Goodreads Review*

"A scorching glimpse of one man's reality. Multifaceted. Buckle up. This is an unflinchingly deranged ride. As close to a perfect depiction of humanity as you may find."

—*Rebecca, Five-Star Amazon Review*

"Poetry at its finest. I've followed the author on Instagram from the beginning. He loves and feels with such intensity."

—*Debbie, Five-Star Goodreads Review*

"Not your typical book of poetry, which is probably one reason I like him so much. He's not afraid to put anything to pen and paper."

—*MLC, Five-Star Amazon Review*

"So beautifully raw."

—*Emma, Five-Star Goodreads Review*

ALSO BY J. WARREN WELCH

POETRY

That's Not Poetry

FICTION

"Caroline"
a short horror story featured in
Witches of the Wood

Your Mom Thinks It's POETRY

J. WARREN WELCH

BIG SMALL TOWN BOOKS

We like to talk
about our moments
such poetic ...
but when I l...
what I hate
every ... ... me

I would rather be
even just moderately
good at being honest
than be the best in the world
at merely using words.

J. Warren Welch

I really don't believ[e]
we will ever run out
of wonderful new thin[gs]
to do to each other.

J. Warren Welch

BIG SMALL TOWN BOOKS

Published by Big Small Town Books,
an imprint of Big Small Town Entertainment.

www.bigsmalltownbooks.com

Formal requests to the publisher may be sent to:

Big Small Town Books
P.O. Box 311
Unicoi, Tennessee, 37692

Reviewers may quote brief passages as part of their reviews.

Paperback ISBN 978-1-7341660-1-9   •   Also available as an eBook.

Cover Designed and Copyright © 2020 Dustin Street. Images courtesy of
Pixabay and @j.warren.welch Instagram. Cover model: Natasha Welch

Printed in the United States of America. This book utilizes the Avenir family of fonts,
as well as Iowan Old Style Roman, Beautiful Heart and Tox Typewriter typefaces.

First Printing: February 2020

10 9 8 7 6 5 4 3 2 1   20 21 22 23 24 25 26

For every snob who decided my ability to connect with a broad audience must mean I'm not a real poet.

Die mad about it.

CONTENTS

Your Mom Thinks It's
POETRY

Don't let that pretty cover fool you.

This is anything but squeaky clean...

FOREWORD

WE HAVE ALL READ the lines of poetry that touch us and make us feel something. Make us feel anything. Within those words, we sometimes find ourselves—or some version of what we perceive our lives and selves to be.

J. Warren Welch takes this want and insatiable need to be understood and lays it down upon his pages like one would lay a lover on a bed. Raw, vulnerable and unapologetic.

Your Mom Thinks It's Poetry takes everything you thought you knew about lyrical rhymes and writing crimes and brings it all together in one intense and intoxicating ink-spread canvas. You will be transported to the edge of your every desire and whim, with J. Warren Welch as your personal guide and muse.

Within these pages, you will be laid bare among the words and covered in emotion and sheer fuckery. If you have ever wanted to feel sexy or seen—or seen as sexy—each and every poem will satisfy that urge.

This book not only expands on the genius and brilliance of *That's Not Poetry*, but entirely blows the mind with its insightfully relatable and skillfully presented content. *Your Mom Thinks It's Poetry* is not just paper between two covers, it is its own show—from curtain to intermission to bows.

J. Warren Welch commands the reader's attention and holds it as a child would cling to the bosom of its mother. The spaces between the words give you pause to contemplate how J. Warren Welch got inside the recesses of your mind and subconscious.

A magician with his art, he will have you disappear into the crevices of every single paragraph and reappear on the other side, completely mind-fucked and transformed.

J. Warren Welch has the professionalism and word formulations of the most renowned writers on the market and shares those impressive abilities with the world. Whether you think it's poetry or not, trust us: your mom *definitely* thinks it is poetry.

Get lost inside the mind and musings of one of the greatest not-poets to ever find a platform. When you are reading the poetry of J. Warren Welch, you are not just scanning lines, you are learning. You are growing. You are becoming a better version of your perceived self, and you will be able to take from his writing specific expressions and cues that will make you a better human all around.

Sometimes a book just understands you without

ever knowing you, and that's the kind of book that makes us believe in love, life and—just maybe—a world that isn't as shitty as we expect it is.

J. Warren Welch brings you out of reality and into an illusion of all we imagine being alive entails. There are times when we read the words within the poem. And then there are times we *become* the poetry.

—S.S. Marshall
 @s.s.marshall

Your Mom
THINKS I'M WISE

In this artificial,
fake-as-fuck world,
the most beautiful,
AROUSING,
and sexy things that exist
are those rare moments
of bare-naked,
RAW,
somewhat filthy,
and often disturbing
HONESTY.

You know what's sexy as hell?

Sweat.

Calloused hands.

Bloody knuckles.

Facing your demons.

Eyes full of tears that still show no sign of surrender.

Hanging on to the end of a rope.

Surviving the fall.

Lifting yourself up from rock bottom.

Beating the odds.

Proving them all wrong.

Never,

Ever,

giving up.

That shit is fucking sexy.

Karma?
The Universe?
The Gods?
None of them
are going to need
any help from you
when the time comes
to tear their pound of flesh
from your guilty bones.
Stop trying to punish yourself.
That's not your fucking job.

Let that shit go.
That's what I do.
That's what I've always done.
But what do you do
when that shit won't let go of you?
That's when you just have to ride it out,
painful as that ride will be.
Feel those feels.
Cry those tears.
Wrestle with that knot in your stomach
that won't let you sleep at night,
until time finally does
what time always does,
and then,
let that shit go.

YOU'VE HAD SOME PRETTY fucked up yesterdays, haven't you? And you may be staring down the barrel of a tomorrow that doesn't look any goddamn better. But right now, in this moment...

Okay, let's cut the crap. Right now feels pretty fucked up too, doesn't it? My Zen is the bastard son of the Dalai Lama and Spartacus.

Breathing in: "Nam Myōhō Renge Kyō."

Breathing out: "Those who are about to die, salute you."

Those contemplative breaths feel more like a desperate labored gasp, and the drum-like thump of my racing heartbeat negates the possibility of ever feeling calm, but I still hold onto them.

Gasp. Thump-thump. Gasp. Thump-thump. Gasp...

No, this probably isn't what enlightenment is supposed to look like, but I could still park my un-enlightened ass on top of a mountain and make motherfuckers climb up there to learn how to survive when "inner peace" is just too far out of reach.

It's a fucking war in there, isn't it? Concentrate on your exhausted breath, and focus on the feeling of your heartbeat pounding against the inside of your ribcage.

Gasp. Thump-thump. Gasp. Thump-thump. Gasp. *You're surviving now, grasshopper.*

You've been running for so long.
Away from what you're certain isn't love,
and toward what you desperately hope might be.
But somehow, in all that running,
through a world full of *someone-elses*,
you never learned how to take
the first fucking step
toward yourself.

Motivated by love
or hate,
they'll try to pull
or push you away
from who you are.
Don't break.
Don't even sway.
With steadfast resolve,
occupy that space
that belongs to you,
and only you.
They can join you there,
or they can run away.

The most dreadful times you face
are the only opportunities you will ever get
to prove to yourself
exactly what you're made of.

You're not getting any younger,
and you're running out of time
to love yourself
the way you've always deserved
to be loved by you.

THE THINGS THAT MADE US

I've been forged by pain—
but we all have, haven't we?
An overused cliché that still somehow rings so
    true
because it's so goddamn universal.
The hell I've been through doesn't make me spe-
    cial, though,
and it doesn't make you special either.
Mere survival of hardship does not make us wor-
    thy
of a trophy or a medal or even a pat on the back.
What did you become?
Are you just like them?
Every user and abuser that molested and infected
your very core?
Did the world create you in its own disgusting
    image?
Or did you resist,
And persist in being something better.
Something hideously pure
and absolutely fucking sure
that you are better.
Better than every lie you've been told
and every counterfeit love you've been sold.

Better than the sum total of all the material they
    used to make you.
I hate every single thing that made me,
but Jesus Christ,
how I love who I am.
I really am special, and so are you.
Because we somehow became something far
    more beautiful
than the pain life put us through.

MOST OF US WHO live with depression, and its many insidious variations, have found our own way to deal with those terrible things that our own head does to us. Whether we do it with medication or without, it still takes an enormous amount of will-power—which, by the very nature of who we are, we possess precious little of.

But we hold it together, day after day, meticulously balancing the pieces of ourselves right where we know they need to be to ensure our own survival.

Inevitably, though—no matter how long we've played this merciless game—at some point, we're going to fall to pieces again.

It might happen from exhaustion, or sometimes it happens because we get just a little too arrogant about how well we're coping, and forget who we really are.

Sometimes it just happens because…well, shit happens. You know?

Then we're left standing in a pile of our own dismantled defense mechanisms, with nothing between us and a very clear reflection of who we really are. Who we've always been. Who we almost certainly will be forever.

This is when every bit of self hatred we've been trying to convince ourselves isn't there smashes down on us like the weight of a thousand planets. And when we need that strength we rely on the most...

It just isn't there.

But this is not where we give up. We've built these walls before, and all the pieces are still right here. I know—the thought of putting all that shit back together for what seems like the millionth time is just...

Goddamn, it's painful. But it's necessary. We will do this now, and we will do it a million more times if that's what it takes.

Why? Fuck, I don't know, but we had a reason at one point, didn't we? If that one doesn't work any more, find another one, or make one up. It doesn't really matter why. It only matters that we keep rebuilding—every time we fall apart.

*What-if*s
only exist
to rob right now
of what is.

You'll never know
if they really love you
if you never show them
who you really are.

After a lifetime
of being too much for some
and not nearly enough
for far too many others,
if you are lucky enough to find,
or be found by,
someone who makes you feel like
maybe you're really just right,
you better make damn certain
that you make them feel the same way.

You're worth more than this
and you know it.
Please stop
quantifying love
in terms of how much hell
you will allow someone else
to put you through.

Don't surround yourself
with people who make you feel
better about who you are.
Surround yourself with people
who make you want to be better
than you ever have been.

WHEN I LOOK AT those I love, my chest gets tight and I want to hold them and cry and apologize for being who I am. They deserve someone more than me. I've never felt like enough, and I think we all feel that way just below the surface.

We're all just consciousness that got dumped into time and space without our consent, and now we're all doing the best we fucking can.

That feeling that we're less than what we should be is just part of the human condition. It's something we all share and none of us knows the cure—because there isn't one.

The thought of others feeling this way hurts as much as feeling it myself, and the only way I know to somewhat alleviate my own delusions of inadequacy is to tell others over and over again that their delusions of inadequacy are wrong.

They are enough.

You are enough.

We are all enough.

Learn to love
the mundane
Again.
Regain that
childlike wonder.
Those little things
you once found exciting
can still give you thrills
if you pretend every time
is the very first time.

Your ability to find
the good in someone else
is not a reflection
of how much good is in you.
Some people are just as toxic
at their core
as they appear to be on the surface.
Don't burn yourself out
trying to see virtue
where it doesn't exist.

You deserve to be happy.
Don't rob yourself of that
just because some of the people around you
will never deserve
a happy version of you.

"You only get one shot."
That's some inspirational,
win-one-for-The-Gipper,
charge-that-hill-sounding shit.
It's also just not true.
Every moment is a new shot.
A small section of time and space
that you can win or lose,
no matter what has happened
in all of your moments before.
Some moments may be more important than others,
but if you can dominate
the seemingly unimportant moments in your life,
bigger moments are going to come your way.
And you'll be ready.
And you better stay ready,
because you're probably going to get
more than one of those shots.

The difference between
a hero and a villain
isn't in their backstory;
it's in their response to their backstory.
Depending on who you ask,
or when you ask them,
I've been the hero
and I've been the villain.
The good news is:
Today is tomorrow's backstory.
And it's never too late
for a major plot twist
in our own story.

No excuses.
Start today,
right where you're standing,
with whatever you have.
Look around.
Find a tampon and a clothes hanger.
Make that shit happen, MacGyver.

Don't become so consumed
with trying to be just like your heroes
that you deprive the world
of the hero you could be.

Every day is another chance.
Every breath is a new opportunity.
These moments aren't wars,
they're just battles.
You're going to win some,
and yes,
you're going to lose some, too.
But none of those victories
or defeats
will define you forever.
Because tomorrow is always on it's way,
and it can redefine you in an instant.
Be ready.

We resist change

because we're afraid it will mean

we'll owe the world

an apology

for who we are

today.

You know that thing you want to do?
That thing you watch other people do?
That thing your heroes do?
Go do that.
But don't do it
like anyone else
has ever done it
before.

They'll swear
they're your friend,
with your enemy
dripping
from their tongue.

Comfort zones are caskets
where the living lie, and practice
being less than alive
before the body dies.

Don't be so goddamn scared
of being hated by anyone
that you end up hiding
every part of who you really are
from someone who could love you.

Your desperate attempts
at self improvement
will always end in disappointment
if you try to skip
the most important step
of self discovery.
How will you know
what needs to be improved,
if you don't even know
who the fuck you are?

You're so much bigger
than they want you to be.
So many more colors
than their blind eyes can see.
Multidimensional beauty
in a selfie world that's 2D.
Boxes are for captives;
smash those walls and run free.

Burn that list you've been keeping
of the people who have done you wrong,
and start a new list
of all the people who have treated you right.
When it comes time for paybacks,
that's the list that will bring you some real joy.

Any dog will stay
if you keep them on a short enough leash.
You'll never know
if they are truly loyal
until you let them off the chain.

A decorated truth
is nothing more
than another beautiful fucking lie.

People who have spent their whole lives
trying to be someone else
will never understand
when you decide to be yourself.

That person,

who wrote those words

that you really needed to hear today,

was probably just

desperately searching

for the words

they really needed to hear

today.

Here's to the realists
who are still stubborn enough
to keep reaching for stars
they know they'll never touch.

FAMILY PORTRAIT

NEVER SAY "CHEESE" IF you don't mean it.

If a picture is indeed worth a thousand words, then you've just lied, a thousand times over, in an instant, and those lies are frozen in time.

Don't allow yourself to be turned into a prop in someone else's facade. Their fake, picture-perfect, Christmas card, JC Penney's catalog "Family".

With your goofy smile and adorable dimples and empty eyes.

You might as well be a cardboard cutout, because that's all you ever were to them. But you are worth so much more, and someone else will see that, even if no one ever has.

You possess a value so much greater than the lie someone else wanted you to be, and something real will find you when you are ready to be real.

So please, trust me on this:

Never say "cheese" if you don't mean it.

They'll drag their claws through
Everything that's **YOU** inside
Then they'll curse your face
When you build a place to hide.

Friends and family.
Fans and followers.
Lovers.
Especially lovers.
If you haven't given them
all the information,
don't wonder why
it sounds like a lie
when you hear them say
they love you.

Find your voice...
Raise your voice...
Build your voice.

Then use your voice
to help others

Find their voice...
Raise their voice...
Build their voice.

Before you take a step,
ask yourself:
"Is this going to leave a
FOOTPRINT
my corpse will be
proud of?"

Most of your friends
are really enemies
performing reconnaissance.

This moment
might not feel like our best moment,
but that doesn't mean
we have to let it dictate
the quality of the moments that follow.

I try to surround myself
with intelligent people.
I like to have my own intellect
challenged and sharpened,
but when I find that intellect
untempered by heart,
I would prefer to spend my time
with a fool who possesses
even the smallest amount of empathy.

You have to be willing
to push some people away
to make room for those
who really want to stay.

Life is too short
to waste it in relationships
where you spend more time arguing
than you do laughing
and smashing nasty bits together.

There's a healthy way
to not give a fuck.
Let's learn how
to stop giving a fuck
about what others think about us,
while maintaining an empathy
that allows us to still
care about them.

First times
only happen
one time.
Pay attention.
You're going to want
to remember this.

Everyone
worth a fuck
that I've ever known
had a big fucking scar
somewhere.

You have to learn
when to shut your fucking mouth,
and open your arms.
Love doesn't need to have all the answers,
it just has to be there.

COMFORT ZONES AREN'T INHERENTLY bad places.

The problem is, all too often, we convince ourselves we can find rest in someone else's comfort zone.

Normalcy is a fine thing for the normal, but it's a slow, painful death for the strange, the odd, and those of us who just aren't quite like those around us.

Most people can be comfortable and content living life like most other people live it, but some of us were born for bigger adventures.

LIFE IS A VAPOR.

You will be gone in the blink of an eye.

One day you're going to wish you still had those moments that you let some toxic motherfucker rob from you.

One of life's
most tragic ironies
is that all of
our most important
decisions
have to be made
before we're
fully prepared
to make
important decisions.

All of

our lives

zig-zag

and

criss-cross

But I never

ever

forget

a connection.

You don't have
to be perfect
to make a
positive difference
in the world.

DON'T WAKE UP IN the same terrible place ten years from now just because you're terrified of what needs to be done today.

MOST DAYS DON'T FEEL like a win for me.

That's why I root so hard for so many other people who are doing so many different things in so many different ways.

Because even when I'm in the depths of my biggest losses, someone I'm rooting for is probably winning big, and I get to win through them.

I am responsible for the way
I allow other people's negativity to affect me.
I am also responsible for the way
my negativity affects others.

Most of my biggest mistakes
have happened because
I was either
letting my emotions
take me for a ride,
or desperately trying
to avoid them.

I've harmed myself so violently,
literally and figuratively,
to distract myself from the pain
that swirls inside me endlessly.

When you make yourself stop,
and take that deep breath,
and drag your mind back
to right here,
and right now,
you're creating a timeout
and giving yourself
a fighting chance
to make the decisions
that you want to make,
rather than letting your feelings
make decisions you may regret later.

I'm mourning the loss
of ten thousand yesterdays
I spent stuck in tomorrow.

I'm far too old
to die young,
but I'll never stop living
as if that's the goal.

What if we decided
to quantify our own worth
based on how worthy
we make those around us feel?

I'm not exactly
swimming in gold coins,
but I do have a surplus
of the things I value most,
and I consider myself
rich as fuck.

You deserve
to be loved.
Make yourself
believe that.

You've got a head,
and you've got a heart.
If you can't figure out
how to make both of them
motherfuckers
work for you,
then you're gonna get
fucked up by life
every goddamn day.

Sometimes I think,
"This is either the best
or worst decision
I've ever made."
Those are my favorite
fucking decisions.

If they wouldn't dream
of having your back,
why the fuck
do you still have theirs?

I never felt truly
ALIVE
until I stopped obeying
dead fucking rules
written by
DEAD
MOTHERFUCKERS.

Your Mom
IS GIVING ME LIFE

I won't pretend
I didn't love
the skin I'm shedding now,
but I'd rather give that up
than remain the same size
forever.

Old habits die hard,
so I'm still standing—
anxiously,
desperately—
holding everything I am
in front of me.
Everything I have to bring
to other people's tables
is spread out in the perpetual audition
that has always been my life,
and the echoes of a million times that I've heard,
"This seat's taken,"
still haven't taught me
to stop trying to sit
where I know I'm not wanted.

"Be yourself," they say.
"It'll be fun," they say.
What they don't tell you
is how the deafening crash
of a thousand doors slamming shut
because you refuse to fit in
sounds a lot like
your own bones breaking.

YOUR MOM THINKS IT'S POETRY

I'll never make it in this town
because I don't love Jesus,
and he don't love me.
And I don't hunt ducks
or give a fuck about UT.

I'll never make it in this town
Because I don't hate the gays,
and they don't hate me.
And I didn't burn a fucking jersey
when a black man took a knee.

I'll never make it in this town
where the tongue that invites you to church
also uses hateful slurs.

I'll never make it in this town,
and I'll probably never get to leave.

EIGHT SECONDS

MY BIOLOGICAL FATHER IS a handsome god-damn man, and that's all I ever got from him—other than my addictive personality, I suppose. Thanks, Daddy.

I've only seen him in person twice since I was about five or six years old. He was blowing through town on work both times, and I suppose he thought a dinner at a steakhouse would make him feel better about never being there.

Maybe he thought it would make me feel better. I never had the heart to tell him I just don't give a shit. Out of all the things that have hurt me in this life, his absence never was one of them. I never felt the need to hate him, or love him. Total indifference is the only emotion I ever remember feeling toward him—and relief that he ran away.

In person, he seems about seven feet tall, but I'm sure if you were to strip him of his black cowboy boots and tall, black cowboy hat, he's probably about five-foot-one, and even smaller on the inside, where the things that make a man a man are supposed to be.

It must be Halloween every fucking day in Texas, and that is probably Reason Number One that

I'm thankful he is not the man who raised me. If he had, I would most likely believe that dressing up like John Wayne was all it took to be a man, too.

I've got a little bit of life under my belt now, and I've developed enough perspective to know that there are always two sides to these kinds of stories. I don't have a clue why he left, and I'm certain I never will, but I do know this: I spent a decade and a half in a loveless marriage, just to stay with my daughters. Even after finding out about ten years worth of infidelity, I tried to forgive it and move on, just for my daughters. I wasn't strong enough to do that, and that's okay, because I know I pushed myself to the goddamn edge of everything I was capable of—out of love for my children.

Whatever his reasons, whoever's fault it was, I know that cowboy didn't fight that hard to stay with me. I'm also sure that the fact he *didn't* made me the kind of man who *would*.

So I suppose I might owe him something for that—and my ridiculous good looks.

I imagine he spent about eight seconds of his life on me, but that's about all you can expect from a cowboy anyway. And the gift of his absence after those eight seconds made me a man that men like him wish they had the courage to be.

Given a choice between
living or dying,
I'm having trouble deciding
which is more terrifying.

I don't belong
anywhere.
I never have,
and I'm old enough now
to know
I never will.
On my strongest days,
I'm able to wear that
Not Belonging
like a badge of honor.
But in those weaker moments
that I can't outrun,
I'd give anything
to fit in,
anywhere.

My step-daughter was supposed to stay
after school five minutes
to complete an assignment.
An hour later, I was still waiting in the car
livid as fuck.

How could she be so goddamn inconsiderate?

Doesn't she know that an hour of my time
is worth a lot fucking more
than an hour of her time
because I'm forty-one goddamn years old
and I've got a lot fewer hours left
than she does?

"It's about time,"
I said dryly,
as she finally
got into the car.

"I've been hiding in the bathroom because I was
    afraid to do my presentation,"
she said.

I just sighed, and gently,
almost cheerfully, replied:

"That's okay. I didn't have anything I needed to be
    doing anyway."

And I meant it.

Because I've never understood anyone
more than I understood her then.
Because I'm forty-one goddamn years old,
and I spend most of my time
wishing I could just fucking hide
in a bathroom.

I always open the mailbox
like it's Christmas morning.
One day my ship will come in.
Life's a lottery:
You've gotta play if you wanna win.
But today it's just more
credit card and medical bills.
And the mail don't run on Sunday
so I've gotta wait till Monday
to play again.

I'm just so fucking tired.
That Exhausted Mind, Body, and Soul
kind of tired,
and I can't wait for the day
that I finally get to take
a nap that I never wake
up from.

I was fucked too young
and I enjoyed it far too much.
Predictably, it turned me into a monster.
The kind of monster
who watches too much porn
and likes it rough
and can only feel love with his dick.
I knew I was a broken man
before most little boys
knew where babies come from.
I've always hated who I am
but I've found solace in the fact
that I never became the kind of monster
who paid that pain forward,
and no one else has to hate themselves
the way I hate myself
because of me.

My Check Engine light
has been mocking me
for three years.
If I put it in park at a red light,
it wont stall.
I've run out of
sides of my mouth to chew on,
but still can't get these fillings fixed.
If you can't pay your medical bills,
they'll take your ass to court.

**Goddamn, I miss
cigarettes
and whiskey.**

It's starting to feel like
there's a lot more life
in my rear-view mirror
than there is on the road
in front of me.
On some days,
that's a terrifying thought;
on others,
it's a relief.

I wish I could sing,
but I can't carry a tune
in a backpack,
or hit a note
with a Louisville Slugger.
I know:
I'm already smart
and handsome.
I've got abs and pecs
and an awesome beard
and a big dick,
but goddamn
I wish I could sing.
Maybe then,
I would love me.

FOR SPITE

"WHY DO YOU SMILE SO MUCH?"

Someone asked my mother this once, and honestly, it was a very fair question. Her life has never been easy. A Midwest girl from Des Moines who went to Catholic school, and then joined the Air Force soon after high school. There, she met a man and got married and had two sons, eighteen months apart, before being left alone to somehow try and raise those two boys into men.

In those few years between my sperm donor running off and my mother getting remarried, she did whatever it took to take care of us. At one point, she would wear ankle weights so she would weigh enough to sell plasma to buy us eggs, which we would cook in a popcorn popper plugged into an extension cord that was running into someone else's window.

Determination and resourcefulness—that woman possesses both qualities in excess.

I've never forgotten her answer to that question—and it has become a bit of a motto of mine, especially in the very difficult times I have had to face in my own life.

"For spite," she said, with a twinkle in her eye and

a smile that seemed to get bigger when she said it.

That's where I get my fire. That's where I get my fight, and my bad fucking attitude. That's where I get my will to live when living just doesn't seem worth it anymore. That's where I get my intelligence and my empathy.

She is also certainly the hereditary source of my depression and anxiety (though she would scold me and say those aren't hereditary) but now that I've mastered the art of smiling through those as well, they seem like precious gifts that I couldn't imagine facing the day without.

Sometimes the closest thing to a "win" you will ever get out of life is in those determined moments, just after life has completely fucked you up, and you are down for the count—but you still find just enough strength inside to stand up and wipe the blood from your lip, and smile your biggest fucking smile through all of the tears and pain that life has piled on you, and say: "Is that all you've got?"

That's how I've made it this far. Out of spite.

And I learned that from the strongest person I've ever known, who taught me that even though I may never win a goddamn thing, if I can keep a smile on my face through everything that life throws at me, I'm sure as shit not ever going to lose.

I want to give up most days.
Surrender's sweet siren song cries out
and everything in me wants to follow.
But I can't,
because I know that I'm built to take everything I
    do too far,
and giving up probably isn't something
that needs to be taken to extremes.
So I keep fighting,
not because I'm brave,
but because I'm scared to death
of what would happen
if I ever did
give up.

In my youth,
I abhorred
the way souls
are bought and sold.
But now I'm old,
and I'm holding
out for better offers.

I'm fairly certain
this is a midlife crisis.
Most of my moments
have the
melancholic sting
of death
hanging over them.
I'm not going to
freak out though.
I'm not going to
buy a Corvette,
or die my gray hair,
but I'm probably
going to start having
a lot more orgies.

I've felt the sting of exclusion
my entire life.
Everyone looks so cozy
in those tiny boxes
that I've never been able to fit into.
But what if I had figured it out?
What then?
What if I had been able
to amputate every strange part of myself
that makes me too big for their small spaces?
I'd hate everything that remained.
So as much as it stings,
I'd rather be all of me,
on the outside looking in,
than be less than what I am,
on the inside with any of them.

MY FATHER'S SON

I SHOVELED THE SNOW off my ex-wife's driveway and porch yesterday. I mean, I needed her shovel for my own driveway, and my daughters live there, but still—I know a lot of men who wouldn't have done that.

It just felt like the right thing to do. I was feeling pretty fucking proud of what a great man I am, then I thought out loud to myself: "Do you know who you are right now? You are your father's son."

Not the cowboy who gave me his DNA and rode off into the sunset. My father. The man who gave me his last name and worked two jobs to take care of my mother and myself and my younger brother.

We don't speak much these days. There's just not any corner of the universe we view the same way, and that's fucking hard for both of us, I think.

I know he loves me, and I hope he knows I love him. I think he knows he could have been a better father. I know I could have been a better son. We both did the best we could. If you were to ask him what it means to be a good man, I promise I would disagree with every thought he has on the subject.

But I didn't learn how to be a man by listening to him. I learned how to be a man by watching him.

The way he pours out all of himself, not just for those he loves and those who love him, but often for people who don't deserve it.

In those moments, when I'm most proud of the man that I am—the way I love, the way I give my-self to others, the way I know how others should be treated, and the way I treat them that way because that's the right fucking thing to do, and good men do the right fucking thing—I can feel him standing there with me.

That's strange, because a lot of who I am is a reac-tion against who he is, but that still doesn't change the fact that I am my father's son.

And I'm glad that I am.

I had no way of knowing
that I was painting myself
into a corner
when I was mind-fucking myself
into loving the darkest
parts of who I am.
I swear to fuck
it was absolutely necessary
for self-preservation,
but I went too far.
And now
that darkness
is the only part
of who I am
that I'm capable of loving
at all.

I'm finally starting to learn
how to sit back and enjoy the ride.
Anticipation used to kill me.
Now it makes me feel alive.

"This is an impressive rap sheet, Mr. Welch."
"Thank you, Your Honor."
I wasn't tryin' to play,
I really just didn't know what to say.
And ever since that day,
the only thing I see when I look at my own face
is every mistake I ever made.
"Don't marry a pre-med student.
Marry a surgeon who's already gettin' paid."
I tell my daughters, then explain:
"Potential don't mean a goddamn thing
if you flush it all away."

Clarity feels heavy,
like a past-due levy imposed
present, of past composed,
and a future foreclosed collide.
Sober-eyed tears undried,
flowing from face, confide regret.
Lifetimes can't be reset,
and attempts to forget fall short.

"RETROACTIVE ABORTION." THAT PHRASE bounces around in my skull on days when my head starts doing those things that I fight really hard to keep it from doing.

It's a different kind of desperation than wanting it all too end. It's closer to wishing none of it had ever started, I guess. It's a longing for the possibility of pulling a Marty Mcfly—going back in time and doing whatever it took to make sure I never happened.

My head decided to go back to that dark place the other day for no real reason. There's never really a reason. It was one of those days where I had my usual, insurmountable to-do list, but I was kicking ass and taking names, as they say. I work well with lists, and I was at the very end of that list.

And then, with nothing left to do but write one more goddamn paragraph for an article that's actually a pretty big opportunity for me, my head just stopped. I didn't want to write. I didn't want to think. I didn't want to breathe. I didn't want to...be.

Those thoughts run through a deep part of me that's completely immune to logic. So when I tried to tell myself things weren't that bad, my self responded with, "It ain't that fucking good, either."

I just had to ride it out. I finished that article a

few minutes ago and I think I'm getting back in my groove. This isn't one of my normal inspirational pep talks. It's also not a cry for help. I'm good, y'all. Really. This is what I do, and I know a lot of y'all go through the same shit, so this is just a "me too."

I don't know why, but it has always helped me to know I'm not the only motherfucker who has to fight these stupid battles. So, hopefully, this will find someone who really needs to know they're not the only one either.

I'M LEARNING THAT I don't have to hate who I used to be just because I like who I am now a great deal. I used to kick down people's doors and take their things. I spent ten years paying off a student loan that I spent entirely on cocaine. I recorded two Christian hip-hop albums. I weighed 123 pounds, and I was snorting pain pills between verses when I recorded the second one.

I voted for Mitt Romney.

There's a lot of stuff in my past that's just fucking embarrassing, and even more stuff that I'm deeply ashamed of. But I'm learning to give myself a little bit of credit because I know I really did do the best I fucking could with what I knew and what I had to work with at the time.

You probably did, too. Sometimes you just can't figure out what the best version of you looks like until you've experienced every single shameful, embarrassing aspect of the worst version of who you are.

That's okay. As long as you learned every lesson that needed to be learned along the way and finally arrived at a place you can be proud of, then don't waste any time hating who you used to be.

You deserve a thank-you for carrying your ass to this point, even if it wasn't always a beautiful journey.

"All eyes on me..."
All the white boys wanted to be
Tupac in the 90s,
and I was an attention whore
long before
I heard that mantra on a beat.
That's just who I am.
It's something sick that I need,
and I'm okay with that,
as long as someone finds
something they need
when their eyes fall on me.

There's a shame
that people who had
very grown-up things
done to them at an early age
carry for the rest of their lives.
You can see the weight of that shame
in their tear-filled eyes,
and hear it in their trembling voices
when they tell their stories.
Stories that sound a lot like mine.
But the only shame I ever felt
was the shame of knowing I never felt
any goddamn shame at all.
The shame of the realization
that I was probably already fucked up
before anyone ever came along
to fuck me up.

Troubled by this plan for us,
birth to dirt, non-stop crisis,
let's pretend it's glamorous,
show more skin; they'll all buy it.
Do life and death coincide
to make our anguish double?
Try as we might to grow inside,
we'll not escape this bubble

Perhaps the gods
are just try'na be funny,
closin' all these doors
like they ain't seen my rap sheet

I've spent years floating
on a bourbon surface,
but now I'm starting to realize
that there are
frightening and fascinating
depths of who I am
that could never be explored
without a clear head.

Do I really have
a low self-esteem,
or is this lifelong
anger and sadness
really the result of a
God-sized arrogance
that gets
super fucking offended
when someone else
doesn't seem to think
I'm as awesome
as I think I am?

I've never had a good dream.
I don't really have many nightmares either.
Most of my dreams are just
frustrating...
But last night I had a dream
where I was standing in a strange room,
surrounded by strange people,
and one of those strange people
offered me a drink,
and I turned around and walked away.
I'm going to call that
a good dream;
and that's a first for me.

Maybe today I won't think about the blade.
Maybe today I won't long for the grave.
Maybe today oxygen won't sting.
Maybe today my head won't do those things.
Maybe today won't be so heavy.
Maybe today I won't feel unsteady.
Maybe today will taste more like hope.
Maybe today this won't be a fucking joke.
Maybe today those demons will rest

for just

one

goddamn

minute

so I can catch my fucking breath...

Maybe tomorrow.

YOUR MOM THINKS IT'S POETRY

Looking at the bright side
hurts my fucking eyes.
I'm always staring into the darkness.
The negative.
The unpleasant.
I'm not good at gratitude or thankfulness
because I'm always wrestling
with things in my mind
that make me anxious and vexed.
But sometimes the reality
of just how far I've come,
and just how much I have
that I really don't deserve,
cuts through all of those negative thoughts like a laser.
Those moments make me happy.
I am the luckiest motherfucker
in the history of motherfuckers.

I'VE CREATED THIS PILE of muscle and ink and facial hair and anointed it with Big Dick Energy. What you see is exactly who I wish I was, but in reality, I still cry very real tears every goddamn time I hear "Mr. Jones" by The Counting Crows.

"Man I wish I was beautiful..."

Beneath what you see, I'm still sixteen, skinny and acned, and just so fucking painfully awkward. My real life Mr. Jones was Mike, and he married the girl of my dreams. One of the girls of my dreams. They were all the girls of my dreams, but none of them ever had a dream about me.

"Man I wish I was beautiful..."

Beneath that, I'm still five, staring down at a plate of eggs covered in ketchup, after giving every bit of my tiny heart and my tiny body away, and having it thrown back in my face.

"Man I wish I was beautiful..."

I tell people not to let just one moment define them for their entire lives, but the truth is: I don't know how the fuck not to do that, because I can still taste her tongue, and those eggs, and that first worst rejection, and I can't figure out how to get up from that fucking table and walk away.

"Man I wish I was beautiful..."

The truly fucked up thing is I'm probably someone else's Mr. Jones today, but when I hear the praise that I so desperately need to feel directed at me, it doesn't change a thing. I've been told I'm beautiful, but I still can't choke down those eggs.

Man I wish I was beautiful...

SMITTY DIED. I'M FEELING a bit emotional about that, which is odd considering the fact that I never knew him, and I thought he was already fucking dead.

His real name was Russell Warren Smith, but everyone called him Smitty. He and my biological father met in the Air Force. Smitty lived with my parents for a while, when they were all stationed in San Antonio.

There was a popular perfume at the time called Smitty, and their slogan was "Smitty did it!" So when my mother got pregnant with me, that became the running joke, because of their living arrangement.

Someone even got my mother a shirt with the slogan on it.

Mother assures me that Smitty certainly did not do it, but it was such a hilarious joke that they decided to give me his middle name. I never knew that part of the story until today, and I've been smiling about it all day.

I don't know what kind of man Smitty was. He was probably a little good and a little bad, just like most of us. Now he's a little dead, and I'm a little part of his legacy in some strange, hilarious way.

We all cause ripples that expand from that small place and time where we landed in the universe, and those ripples will continue to affect the world in big ways and small ways, for better or worse, long after we're gone.

To the extent that I can control the effect of the ripples I leave, I hope they're really fucking big, and I hope they makes lives better. I want that to be my legacy, and then it'll be Smitty's legacy too.

I never tried
to wash what you did to me
off of me.
I just wanted to soak
in that delicious sin
forever.
Now,
half a lifetime later,
I'm still drowning
in you.

I prefer the written word
because it allows me
to be completely honest
while feeling as safe as a liar.

I miss Jack Daniel's and Colt 45.

I miss Marlboro Reds and feeling alive.

I miss cocaine, and Xanax, and Lortab highs.

Sometimes when it's really bad, I even miss Jesus
Christ.

Because right now, every single bit of life

is crushing what's left of whatever's behind these
eyes,

and even just the smallest fucking crutch

would be really goddamn nice.

I keep getting these signs from the universe.
Don't tell me how stupid that sounds.
I know how fucking stupid that sounds,
but these signs keep telling me
that no matter how much I doubt myself
and question everything I'm doing,
I'm doing what I'm supposed to be doing,
and I need to keep doing it.
I don't know why,
and I don't know what's going to happen,
but I'm going to listen to the universe,
and just keep doing what I'm doing—
Even if that does sound fucking stupid.

I REMEMBER BEING VERY young and overhearing some adults talk about suicide. Even at that early age, my first thought was "You can do that? That's an option?"

I've been fighting that thought ever since. Some of us just have heads that work like that, I think. It was slightly easier to fight during the lengthy parts of my life, when I wrapped myself in a religion that made me feel like there was some sort of meaning or virtue in that fight.

Now, I don't believe in any of those things anymore, so when my emotions scream out "This is all so fucking pointless!" my intellect answers with "Well, you're not wrong."

But I still fight those thoughts, and I try to be here for others who are fighting the same thing every single day.

Some of us are hurting.

Some of us are trying to help the hurting.

Some of us are doing both at the same goddamn time, and if we all do the best we can, for ourselves, and for those around us, some of us might fuck around and live a good long life, in spite of what our heads try to do to us.

I've smashed my fists
against walls of stone
then blamed those walls
for my broken bones.

Throw your self-righteous stones
My flesh is torn, but bones unscathed
The road to hell is paved
With haughty looks down saints' noses
Faux Jesus Christ poses
All thorns and no roses beneath
I'll turn the other cheek
And grind my sinner's teeth for flames

The faintest threads of light
are starting to break through
pinholes
in the walls I've built around myself.
Even the slightest brightness is blinding,
and my eyes burn trying to readjust.
This darkness feels like home.
It feels like familiarity
and safety.
But maybe
I don't really want to die
having never seen
the light of day.

The sands of time pile high
Hourglass bubble alive with death's song
That weakens our headstrong
Denial of how wrong we've lived life
Impending night grants sight
But leaves no time to right transgressions
Funeral processions
Don't stop for confessions a day late

I've got a lot of fucking nerve
talking about the unhealthy ways
that men view women
for a man who can only see the world
in flesh tones,
and sees a potential orgy
in every crowded room,
and doesn't give a fuck
where he goes when he dies
as long as there is
FUCKING
there.

Daytime's frantic thoughts
lead to nighttime's frantic dreams.
Not a moment's peace.

I don't believe love is finite.
I don't believe you can ever run out
of love to give,
no matter how much
you give it away.
But even if it were an exhaustible resource,
I know I'm just getting started,
and I've barely scratched the surface
of how much love
I was put here to share.

Do you remember that time
when you could have stood up for me,
but you didn't want to pick sides?
I DO.
And I *always* will.

I will do as much
as time and anxiety
allow me to do.

I watched my daughter sing
at someone else's daughter's funeral,
and I marveled at the heart's ability
to burst with pride
and break
all at the same time.

THERE'S NOTHING I WOULDN'T do for those I love. Just point me at the problem. Oh yeah, we can break that. Or burn it down. Or kick its ass. I got you.

But when the problem is grief, and there's nothing I can destroy to make it better? Fuck. I got nothing. I can't help. I'm useless. Every word I say in those situations sounds far more cold and calloused than I mean for it to sound, but that's how I get through times like that, and it's the only fucking trick I know.

I can get really fucking cold really fucking fast when I know my self-preservation depends on it.

All of my emotions are tied to switches in my chest and my go-to defense mechanism is the ability to flip those motherfuckers on and off at will.

But most people aren't made like that, and I don't know how to help. "Just stop feeling." That's what I want to say, because that's what I do, and it always makes it worse when I say it.

So I'm sorry I'm like this, and I'm sorry it hurts. Feel what you need to feel, in the way you need to feel it, for as long as you need to feel it. Pour all of those tears on me till they finally run dry. I know I can't help, but I'm still right here, and I always will be.

I'd rather be a breathing disappointment
Than a dead inspiration

    So I'll take my pill that makes me feel
    Not quite right, but less ready to die
    And I'll drink this forty in my basement
    And expose my lies, and face them

Because I haven't wanted to die
For more than a few consecutive nights
And no one knows how close I was…

Knife-on-my wrist close
Same-lane-as-a-logging-truck close
Look-at-all-this-fucking-rope close

So right now I know a lot's not right
But I'm terrified
To try to make anything right

Because for the first time
In a long fucking time

I KIND OF LIKE BEING ALIVE

Facebook says
we have ninety-four mutual
  friends.
That probably means
I have less friends
than I think I do.

Your Mom
THINKS IT'S POETRY

You brought pretense to a battle of charisma. How's that workin' out?

YOUR MOM THINKS IT'S POETRY

My words are for the broken.
The freaks and the perverts.
The junkies and drunks.
The misunderstood,
who struggle to understand themselves.
The ones who aren't sure they would swerve
if death was barreling toward them.
The ones who somehow simultaneously
care way too goddamn much
while not giving a single fuck.
I write for those who know how to laugh
to keep from crying,
and how to cry
without giving up on trying.
If what I'm doing,
and the way I do it,
doesn't feel like it's for you,
then consider yourself blessed.
But I didn't drag myself this far
to turn my back on the distressed.

If you love poetry, don't try to lock it in a cage.

Have you ever been "loved" like that?

I have, and it was a fate far worse than being hated.

Let poetry be what it needs to be to make it through
the day.

Let it be 150 lines, and let it be 3.

Let it be monsters and demons, and let it be a "she."

Let it be a fairytale and lost love's sadness.

Let it be beautifully broken fire and chaos and mad-
ness.

Let it be beard oil and flannel and whiskey and
typewriter ink.

Let it be the millionth second coming of the same
    goddamn poet from The Beat.
Let it be an ex-con who will spend the rest of his
    life trying to prove
that he is somehow something more than his rap
    sheet would show to you.
If you really love poetry, you have to let it be a
    cliché,
because at the end of the day, that's all the fuck
    we all are anyway.
If you haven't poured enough of yourself out to
    understand
that you are also just another clone,
that probably means you're the kind of cliché
that sits in a glass house and throws stones.

REAL POETRY

SHE COULDN'T HAVE WEIGHED a whole ninety pounds. I think she said she was in her late 20s, but time had had its way with her, and her eyes told the story of many more years than that.

She stood in front of our 12-step group and told her story. This was long before "trigger warnings" were a thing...and there just wouldn't have been enough anyway.

I'd never heard anything like it.

I'm a sensitive guy, but I have never cried as much about someone else's life as I did listening to what she had lived through. I'm talking about the kind of crying that less jaded folks than myself do at funerals.

Her honesty...goddammit.

I had never seen anything like it.

She told her story with a confidence that broke through the quiet timidity of someone that you could tell was just waiting for the next fucking blow. She was not an intelligent woman, and I very seriously doubt she knew how to read or write. But to this fucking day, I have never seen a more perfect representation of what real poetry looks like.

And I doubt I ever will.

They've beaten this horse
so far beyond death—
Definition by subtraction,
till they're the only ones left.
These battles are beneath me,
but I don't intend to lose.
Because they're not really judging me.
They're judging you
for enjoying
whatever the fuck it is
that I do.

Color me unimpressed.
You haven't moved me yet to tears.
Pounding poetic chest
Won't reach beneath to rest my fears

I love the way
your condescending face
looks at me like
I'm auditioning for a place
at your table.
That expression is sure to fade
when I take your fucking table
and just walk away.

Without the wisdom
to know when the fight
has finally been won,
the underdog
will keep fighting
in the same
ferocious manner
and may quickly become
the bully
without
realizing it.

I'M CLOSER TO A Kardashian than a Kerouac. I know that. Just because I'm not a literary genius doesn't mean I'm a fool who lacks self awareness.

I really did start all of this with the noblest of pretentious intentions. I wanted to be a real artist. An artist respected by other artists.

What I soon learned, though, is that art is more about what you hide from your audience than what you show them, and I've been hiding almost everything about myself from everyone around me for far too long to live like that any more—privately or publicly.

I have plenty of dark days full of deep thoughts that are just sullen enough to be considered artistic, I suppose. And on those days, I share those thoughts.

But you know what? Those are my very worst days. Those are the days I don't think I'll make it. Those are the days I don't even want to make it.

On a good day, though, my thoughts are short and trite and lack depth and start with a "she" and end with a joke about streaming porn.

Good days look like a grown-ass man dancing in unicorn leggings in front of a squat rack. Good days look like the kind of days real artists don't show you, because good days are never "serious" days and **art is fucking serious...**

So maybe I'm not an artist.

Or maybe I'm only an artist on my worst days, and that's just going to have to be okay, because those really good days full of vapid thoughts are what keep me from drawing a warm bath and grabbing a razor blade.

And I'm going to celebrate every goddamn one of them.

I don't bow my head to deities
or pledge allegiance to nations.
I'm sure as shit not about to worship
a dead fucking poet.

That's a nice
paradigm
you've got there.
It would be a shame
if someone
            sh i f te d
                    i t .

Poetry is not dead
Bukowski is, though
Get off his dick.
He's fucking dead.
That's just fucking gross.

Paradigms exist for shifting.
Dogmas pray to be razed.
Boxes long for wrecking balls.
Rules left unbroken breed malaise.

Once binding dogmas eviscerated
Unmuzzled mouths are prone to sedition
Threats of a nonexistent perdition
Created to keep us subjugated

Poets and Priests would have us sedated
Breaking our will with skillful attrition
Commandments designed to kill ambition
Uniqueness must not be tolerated

I don't possess knees that bend to bow down
To Gods nor humans who try to guard gates
I'll build my own throne and fashion a crown
Then you can bow down to something you hate

Pompous and arrogant self righteous clowns
Waste prayers for the day that I'll abdicate

YOUR MOM THINKS IT'S POETRY

Maybe you're right.
Maybe our culture is just fucked.
Maybe there's too many reality stars
taking too many selfies
with too many filters.
Maybe a hundred years ago
people would have been smart enough
to give you the attention
you are certain you deserve...
But maybe if you really cared
about improving our culture,
and you really are as brilliant
as you swear you are
you could figure out
how to engage this culture as it is
and possibly improve it
in some small way,
rather than longing for a culture
that doesn't exist anymore
and probably wouldn't have
fallen at your feet to worship
the way you think they would
anyway.

They fill every inch
of the page.
I think they're probably
AFRAID
of what those blank
spaces might say.

I WON'T PRETEND THAT I could ever possibly understand what it must feel like to be born in a body that you know just doesn't belong to who you are.

But I do understand exactly what it feels like to be hated for nothing more than being who I know that I am.

And I will always be on your side.

About once a week or so,
I treat myself to three orders
of biscuits and gravy
after I drop the girls off at school.
There's always a group of old men
drinking coffee and talking in the corner.
They're usually talking about old cars,
but today they were pontificating about
"what's wrong with the world these days."
Apparently, all of our problems
are caused by marijuana,
too many brown people,
and not enough guns.
I'm starting to think that wisdom
isn't a byproduct of age after all.

TO THE YOUTH

I'M AN OLD MAN, and right now a lot of old men and women are trying to tell you to sit down and shut up about things that matter to you. You're too young. You're too emotional. You lack the maturity for these grown-up conversations. Go eat your Tide Pods and play with your fidget spinners and use words in strange contexts that we don't understand. We'll take care of the world's problems.

Except we won't.

We've proven we're not capable of doing that. Look around. We made this, and there's not one single thing we can point to in it as evidence that we have any fucking idea what in the actual hell we are doing.

We have failed, but you don't have to.

Raise your voice and refuse to be silenced—by anyone. Do you have all the answers? Probably not. But maybe you have time to find them if you start looking now. Your views will probably evolve and change as you get older, but that doesn't mean that what you believe passionately right now doesn't have any value.

The pride of years lived makes us want to hold on to this disgusting world we've created, but we don't deserve it anymore. You need to take it from us. Right now. Before we fuck it up even more than we already have.

I don't think you will find it at all difficult to do a better job than we have done.

CONSENT IS THE MINIMUM

WE'VE BEEN HAVING THIS intense conversation about consent for a while now, and some of you guys are starting to get it. It's taken time, but a lot of you finally figured out what a two-letter word like **NO** means. And sometimes, you can even get a **YES** in the form of an "Okay...you can put it in me."

Congratulations, pumpkin. You've mastered the not-so-fine art of getting laid without catching a fucking charge. If you think you deserve a high five for that, you're a pretty basic motherfucker.

Manufacturing consent is not the holy grail of male sexuality. Consent is the minimum. Why would you settle for an "Okay" when "Goddammit, If you don't fuck me right now, I'm going to fucking die" sounds so much sweeter?

The goal is lust and passion. The goal is for her to want you so bad it changes the way her goddamn laundry smells. If there is even a fucking question about consent, you need to step up your mother-fucking game.

When she's so attracted to you that she has dreams that look a lot like nightmares about the things she **NEEDS** you to do to her body, you're not going to have to worry about consent.

That's just the way I've always looked at it. But maybe that's not the norm. Because if it were, we wouldn't have to spend so much time defining two-letter words.

I CALL MYSELF A feminist, and I mean that in every way that the word is generally defined. But I've also come to a realization that, for me, it's going to have to have a broader meaning than the one a lot of people associate with the term.

I have three daughters who spend more time with their mother than they do with me. All three of them are deeply religious, and I played a big part in raising them that way before I abandoned such things.

They have never had religion forced upon them, though. Not by me, nor by their mother. That's just who they are right now, and it might always be that way.

My oldest is dead-set on being a missionary. That's what kind of heart she has. Would I rather see her be a CEO? Yes. Yes I would. But guess what? My opinion of the kind of woman she should be is completely irrelevant. That's not my job as a parent, or as a feminist.

My job is to love her, and to make sure that whatever she becomes, it is because that is what SHE wants to be. I want my daughters to feel empowered to be WHO THEY ARE, and if that means going into the mission field, or being a housewife with too many kids, or whatever fulfills THEM—THAT is the life I want for them.

Happiness doesn't look the same to all of us. Not for women, not for men. And all I want for them is to be happy. Whatever that looks like, I will support them completely.

That's what being a feminist means to me.

IT IS NOT GETTING more difficult to be a man in our culture. It's getting EASIER.

We are tearing down the tired, played out, one-dimensional, one-size-fits-all cliche that has defined masculinity for far too long, and with that suffocating box demolished, men are free to be whatever versions of themselves they want to be.

You can be "macho" in the traditional sense, or perhaps a bit more sensitive if that's who you are. I feel most comfortable when I'm able to strike some sort of balance between the two, but that's just me, and that's the beautiful thing: You don't have to be like any other man anymore!

Be the kind of man that YOU are. It's so easy now!

You know what really is getting more difficult to get away with? Being a douchebag. So if you're feeling a little confused and bewildered and a bit frightened to be who you are these days, it's not because you're a man, it's probably just because you're a fucking douchebag.

Love is love,
and far too many people
never find it.
If you do find it,
I am happy for you
beyond what I can express.
I don't care what your gender is.
Or theirs.
I don't care who you fuck
or how you fuck them,
because that's not love.
That's just a part of it.
Love is love
and far too many people
never find it.

THEY BABBLE ON AND on, certain they are impressing me with their knowledge of politics, or religion, or whatever the fuck they are talking about right now.

I don't hear a single fucking word. I just nod and smile and remember that one time–or two, or more, usually–that they pulled that classic, chicken-shit, white person move, where they looked around, leaned in close, and, almost in a whisper, said the N-word.

It happens all the time around here, and every time it does, my mind instantly labels that person, forever, as someone whose opinions–on any and all issues–are never to be taken seriously.

The fact that they would say that word at all tells me everything I need to know about their mind and their heart. The fact that they would assume I wouldn't mind, because of the color of my skin tells me everything I will ever need to know about how they view the world.

All the rebels are dead.
Now we just **dress** like
rebels instead,
and say the **same shit**
a real rebel already said.
In lockstep
we pop Percocets
with whiskey shots next,
and cigarettes
make us feel
like something real
lives in our chest.
We're better than you
because **we're rebels**
just like all the rest.

I DON'T REMEMBER IT being a "thing" when I did it.

There wasn't anyone trying to raise awareness of the fact that this acned, insecure, unstable grunge kid liked to find quiet places and cut himself with razor blades, and to brand himself with cigarettes and chisels heated up red-hot on stove eyes.

I honestly don't even remember where the idea came from. I didn't know anyone else who did that shit.

In my mind I thought, "If I can hurt myself more than anyone else can, then I'm in control. I win."

I branded the word **HERETIC** into my calf with a spoon handle to get back at my minister father. I sure showed him...

Later, when I sang in metal bands, I would slice my torso on stage while I was singing to the point that there was so much blood, people thought it was fake.

At some point, though, I had a thought: it seemed like every force in the universe only existed to **HURT ME**.

And I'll be goddamned if I'm going to do their fucking job for them.

GUYS...HOW DO I say this delicately and con-structively?

STOP. BEING. FUCKING. DOUCHEBAGS.

Every goddamn day, I read multiple social media posts from women about inappropriate messages they've received from men. And on most days, I fucking see it with my own eyes in their comments.

And don't even get me started on the unsolicited dick pics! What the fuck is that?! Are you so stupid that you don't realize you are the Internet equiva-lent of a pervert in a raincoat?

Look. I get it. You see a pretty woman and your dick starts acting crazy. There's nothing wrong with that. God made dicks to do such things.

But I'm the horniest motherfucker on this **PLAN-ET** and I can still handle that shit without sexually assaulting (that's what the fuck it is) women in their inbox!

I am constructed entirely of filthy, inappropriate thoughts, and I have **NEVER ONE TIME** acted like you little boys.

Get a fucking grip. Go rub one out, and act like a fucking man.

WE ARE ALL UNITED now. Again. For the next twenty minutes or so, at least.

Another global group hug in the aftermath of unspeakable atrocities.

But why are we so incapable of sustaining that unity without the umbrella of tragedy to huddle under together?

Soon, the blood will all be cleaned up, and the bodies laid to rest, and the streets swept clean. And we will go back to business as usual. The same sick little seeds that grow in people's hearts and cause them to do these sorts of things will lead us all back to the softer, socially acceptable forms of hatred that we practice every single day.

Towards people who don't pray like we do, or vote like we do.

Towards those who don't look like we do, or fuck like we do.

Towards those who have more, and those who have less.

Even towards people who don't dress like we do, or listen to the same kind of music.

Make no mistake: the very same fear of those who are different than us—the fear that makes people commit acts of terror—also makes those of us who are too civilized to act like that think terrible thoughts about those we disagree with on a daily basis.

We do not murder, but we hate just as passionately.

And that is why the world will never change.

They're so sick
of all of your
attention-seeking selfies
on social media.
So they type up a rant.
To post on social media.
To get attention.
Oblivious to the irony.

I SWEAR TO FUCK I'm not as deeply anti-religion as it seems. My views about such things are based on some very personal experiences, but if your belief in things that I am just completely incapable of ever believing again actually helps you to be the kind of person who shines even just a minuscule amount of light onto the surface of this dark, pointless rock we are all sharing, then I will support you with a million *Amens*.

For fuck's sake! I've cleared out my living room for two Muslim men to say their prayers in my home, and I don't believe in their god any more than I believe in the one I walked away from. But I do still believe in good people—as irrational as that belief feels at times. It's a vibe I get from folks—one that can neither be faked nor hidden, and it exists entirely separate from the beliefs they wrap themselves in.

I'm not anti-religion at all when I see it wrapped around good people. It's the monsters who try to cloak themselves in holy wool that make my eye twitch like a twerking stripper full of the spirit.

TO MY DAUGHTERS

I LOVE YOU, AND I'm proud of each one of you. I'm proud of the young women you are now, and I'm proud of the women that I can tell you are going to be in the future. You each have your own very different and distinctive personalities, but there is a thread of similarity that runs through all of you. That similarity is in your caring hearts, and the enormous amount of empathy you all possess. It's not only apparent to me, but to everyone you come in contact with. That's the sort of thing that should make any parent proud of their offspring.

You all know as well as I do that I won't be winning any **Father of the Year** awards anytime soon. I've certainly not been a *terrible* father, but not a great one either. Just good. Average, maybe? You've had to witness me fight some demons that I'm just now starting to find some sort of victory over.

I also know I've been distant—in a way that men like me try to blame on our "artistic personalities." But it's really just selfishness, if we're being honest. It's hard to love someone else the way you should when you're always just a little too wrapped up in yourself.

There is one thing I feel like I'm getting right,

though, and that is in the fact that I'm not trying to mold you into a new or "better" version of myself. I'm not trying to turn you into the person I want you to be. I'm not trying to choose your path in life for you. Figuring out who **YOU** are is the biggest challenge you will ever face in life, and it is a challenge that is made far more difficult than it should be when parents and relatives—and later in life, friends and love interests—try to influence you in various ways to be the person THEY think you should be.

For all of my shortcomings as a man and as a father, I really do love you girls more than I could ever express, and the only thing I want for you is for you to be happy. There is no happiness in trying to live up to other people's expectations, and I promise you will never have to live up to some sort of vision of who you need to be that I have created in my mind for you.

It is an honor to watch you figure yourselves out, and I honestly can't think of a single time when I thought one of you desperately needed my guidance on an important issue. I love the conversations we have about these things, though. I love to hear the way your minds wrap around these sorts of subjects. I love the way you listen intently when I tell you my point of view, even though we both know my opinions will almost never have any similarity to yours.

I love how we're all okay with those differences.

Just between you and me, girls, this doesn't sound like what most people think of when they think of parenting at all, does it? Maybe I'm too passive. Maybe I'm still being distant and I'm just trying to rationalize it. Maybe I should be working harder to mold you and change you and control you and turn you into...*what, exactly?*

I'm not sure.

Maybe other parents have to do that sort of thing because they weren't lucky enough to have you girls as children, Or maybe their children are just as amazing as you all are, but for some reason they can't step back from trying to change them long enough to see it.

I suppose I'll never know. I am not other parents, and you are not other children.

Only time will tell how you ultimately view me as a father, but I will always consider myself a blessed man to have each of you as a daughters.

I've only ever tried to give you enough space to be yourself, no matter what that meant for you.

But most of the world is not going to be willing to show you that same courtesy. They will try to change you and shrink you down to a size that fits in a box they are more comfortable with. If you learn just one thing from me—if you heed just one piece of advice, please let it be this:

Never allow yourself to be changed into something you are not. Not for anyone. Not for any reason.

You are all beautiful and perfect humans just the way you are. That doesn't mean you're not going to grow and change as you get older, but always do so on *your* terms—not anyone else's.

I love you, and I always will.

Now go figure out who you are.

I know you're going to be really good at it.

WE'RE ALL JUST TRYING to catch those **feels**. That seemingly magical combination of outward stimuli and hormonal reactions that contort our face and make our mouth turn up at the edges.

Different things, or combinations of things, do it for each of us.

It can be love, or sex, family, friends, religion, nature, fantasy, or the warm glow of a smartphone screen.

Whatever it is, there is absolutely no biological difference in the way it affects us—between "real life" and "fantasy."

Ultimately, none of it holds any real or lasting value whatsoever.

So do what makes you feel happy, as much as possible, before the day comes when you will feel no more.

But don't be a fucking snob who thinks the shit that gets you off should be the same shit that gets everyone else off.

It doesn't work like that.

HE POLISHES HIS STATE Championship sporting trophy from high school, and then sets it on the mantel, next to his bowling league trophy from last week.

"Participation trophies! That's why all these goddamn millennials are such fucking pussies," he mumbles to himself.

One old guy to another, I really want to tell him that the worms are going to find my corpse just as delicious as his, even though I've never won anything.

I'm not going to do that, though, because I can tell by the way he looks at that little guy with the bowling ball that he doesn't possess the mental toughness it takes to wake up every day and face a world where his trophies don't mean a goddamn thing.

I'M PRETTY SURE I'M a nihilist.

That's what it really boils down to. At the end of the day, I don't really believe that anything—or any-one—really matters at all.

We are nothing more than animated worm food, sharing a sad, painful journey to an inevitable grave.

I'm not even an atheist. I'm too old and too ex-hausted to care that there are people who believe in something bigger than us, and I don't feel the need to try to take that from them. Honestly, I envy them a great deal.

But I still have this annoying, nagging little voice, that rises up from somewhere in my ribcage, that tells me that, what people **really** need—all people—is a hug.

Just a hug.

The embrace of another traveler on this frighten-ing path we all have to take.

And I refuse to believe that if a selfish, drunken, piece of shit like me can feel such a thing, it's not a universal part of the human condition.

So, if you have wrapped yourself in some sort of worldview or religion or faith that is stifling that voice, I suggest you disrobe yourself of those things immediately, lest you live an entire life, without ever knowing what it feels like to be **ALIVE**.

"It's the LAW!" they scream
With clenched fists and red faces.
"Our nation is the greatest.
Throw those children in cages!"
Then they take a summer break,
To go to far away places,
And somehow keep a straight face
When they tell the children about **GRACE**.

I dropped my daughters
off at school today
and had to wonder
if they were safe
because this is the
U-S-of-fucking-A
and one day
their lives might be the price
that has to be paid
to protect your right
to feel like John Wayne

This is a brutal world,
and those fight-or-flight instincts
run through the core
of every single one of us.
I don't remember a time
when I wasn't lashing out.
My preemptive defense mechanisms
push everyone away
to a safe distance.
But who's going to change this world
into a less brutal place
if every one of us
pushes everyone else
too far away to touch?

BE KIND

When they call the cops on your skin

JUST BE KIND

When those cops yell "don't resist!"

BE KIND

When they call you an "it"

JUST BE KIND

When they tell you where you can shit

BE KIND

When they grab you by the pussy

JUST BE KIND

When your rapist walks free

BE KIND

When they build a wall to stop you

JUST BE KIND

When they elect a man who mocks you

BE KIND

When they drone bomb your kids

JUST BE KIND

When they call you a terrorist

BE KIND

When they decide who you're allowed to marry

JUST BE KIND

So the privileged don't have to worry

If this medication works
I won't
kill myself
before a
white boy
with hate in his heart
and a
semi-automatic
in his hands
gets the chance
to **do it for me.**

Your Mom
THINKS WE'RE
#RELATIONSHIPGOALS

I'll never try to keep you,
but I'll try to be
the kind of place
that makes you
always want to stay.

I told you
I will hold you
without ever
trying to own you,
but that doesn't mean
it won't hurt like hell
if you ever
walk away.

What if I don't need
you to belong to me?
What if you
just continue to belong
to you
and spend a lot of
your time
with me?

I suspect
You only wish
To harm me.
But I've been harmed before,
And these dimples still grab attention.
Bring it on.

There's a special kind of conceit
A lie that most of us believe
That tells us that we
Should be
The only person someone else needs
For eternity

If you can't call it

FREEDOM

Then don't call it

LOVE.

A relationship
shouldn't be about
who can take the most—
Unless you're playing
with a double-ended dildo.
Then it's totally about
who can take the most.

No one ever understood us
before we were together,
and it doesn't really matter
if anyone ever understands
what we have together.

I don't really know how to love.
I'm too selfish,
and I'm already
far too deeply,
passionately,
madly in love
with hating myself,
to know how to love someone else.
But I'm learning,
slowly,
by watching the way
that she loves me.

You're going to have to jump,
and I can't do it for you,
but I'll be here to catch you
if you do.

ON THE THIRD DAY after we started talking, my work computer prompted me to change my password.

I typed in *Natasha01* and mocked my own naiveté aloud. "It's been three days and she's your password now?"

I've always been that person who falls too hard too fast because I just needed to be loved so goddamn desperately; and there I was again, apparently incapable of learning any lessons in life or heeding the advice of the many people who always warned me about the dangers of being such a hopeless fucking romantic.

Today, my work computer prompted me to change my password. It's still her name, years later, with a substantially larger number after it. And every time I type it out, I'm reminded of what a silly, naive, hopeless fucking romantic I am.

And I don't regret that for a single second.

YOUR MOM THINKS IT'S POETRY

The world had become
a deafening wall of white noise,
where everyone sounded
just like their favorite song.
Clones
of copies
of counterfeits,
singing along
to someone else
who was singing along
to someone else's song.
I wanted to stab my own ears
rather than force them to hear
another cover of a cover
of a cover of another
melody that didn't even move me
the first time I heard it.
Then I heard you,
and I fell in love with your song,
because it didn't remind me
of anyone else
at all.

Pinky promise

For as long as you're breathing
I'll fight this urge to stop
with every
fucking
thing
I've got.

Old photographs
remind me
of all the moments
we should have been
together

What if she never
reads the words I write for her?
I want her to know.

Her heartbeat quickened,
and her chest tightened with anxiety
as she typed a message to her husband,
to tell him she'd run into an old friend.
A male friend.
And they went and got coffee,
and caught up.
"Oh that's cool!"
was all he replied.
"You're not angry?"
she asked,
because that's how life had always been
with everyone else.
"Of course I'm not angry.
You are a grown-ass, free woman."
Because that's how love is supposed to feel,
and she's still trying to get used to it.

We both know I'm lying
when I say I'll always love you.
Because I don't believe in always,
and the thought of a forever
where I never get
to finally just
not exist
is terrifying.
I guess what I really mean
when I say that is:
I want to milk this small piece
of definitely-not-forever,
that I get to spend with you
for every goddamn moment I can get.

She interrupted

my morning meditation,

and I finally felt closer to

GOD.

PEOPLE FREQUENTLY ASK MY wife and me what our relationship "secret" is.

I have one answer every time: one hundred percent honesty, and zero percent jealousy.

That's what I say—and then I just want to cry. It's not that it's not the truth, it's just not the whole truth. If that were all it took, I could write myself a bestseller that would put the Good Book to shame, and make a lot of people very happy, and make myself filthy-fucking rich in the process.

There's one more thing you're going to need, though:

A lot of fucking *luck*.

I don't believe in fairy tales, Santa Claus, Bigfoot, Saviors, Destiny, or Fate, and I sure as shit don't believe in soulmates. But do you know what's going to happen to your one-hundred-percent-honest-zero-percent-jealous ass if you allow yourself to be that vulnerable with the wrong person?

You're going to get used up and left for dead, motherfucker. And you'll end up even more cynical than you already are.

So what's the answer, then?

I already told you. One hundred percent honesty and zero percent jealousy—and that's the truly terrifying part.

It takes courage to be that open, knowing what will probably happen to you—again.

I'm not talking about the kind of charge-that-hill courage that can be easily manufactured by a win-one-for-the-Gipper speech and a song about a flag.

I'm talking about a bravery borne out of a desperate, end-of-your-rope readiness to die that runs so goddamn deep you can almost taste the embalming fluid, and smell that sweet soil that you wish would cover you up sooner, rather than later.

It's a giving up—and a giving of absolutely no fucks.

I guess that is the dirty little secret of our relationship. It just wouldn't have happened if we hadn't both been in the same magically terrible place where we just didn't care enough to hide anything from anyone anymore. We didn't care what might happen to us if we were vulnerable. Our honesty was not a virtuous honesty—it was a fucking dare to the whole world: "This is me. Deal with it."

Likewise, our lack of jealousy did not come about because we had had some sort of epiphany that made us realize how toxic jealousy is in a relationship. We were just too goddamn tired to worry about owning, or being owned, by someone else.

You want someone else? Go the fuck on then. We were invincible, because we didn't give a shit anymore, and that feeling of invincibility made us free to open up and love with reckless abandon. And then we got luckier than any two motherfuckers have ever been, and our very sad, random, fucked up paths intersected at just the right time.

Like I said: I don't believe in soulmates. But maybe you don't have to believe in such a thing to find it.

Either way, be brave, be honest, don't be jealous—and maybe you'll get just as lucky as we did.

I'm sorry
for every time
I let myself lose sight of
the fact
that loving you
was always going to be,
and always will be,
**the most important
thing I'll ever do.**

It's hard
to continue to believe
that everything is random
when you find yourself
right in the middle of something
that feels exactly like

PURPOSE.

That moment
after a
long
slow
soft
kiss
where you both gasp for air
and you're so close
that your lungs
are competing
for the same oxygen...

I love that moment.

I'VE ALWAYS HAD THIS Spartan view of love. As if, by fighting enough battles, or jumping through enough flaming hoops, I would somehow achieve "True Love" – that elusive creature I had desired for so long.

I tortured myself with this form of romantic masochism for over a decade. I really thought that by reading all the "Love Is a Decision" and "Love Dare" books, I could work hard enough for her to finally love me and—honestly—for me to finally love her.

I used to make myself feel somewhat noble about it by telling myself it was "for the kids."

But there's really nothing noble about that.

It was already over. In a major way. Long before my naive ass realized it. And no amount of gladiator-like bravery or "hard work" was ever going to save it.

But then I found it. Or it found me.

We found each other somehow. In this random, fucked up universe.

And I've realized something: **Love is NOT work.**

I do not feel like I have to earn anything, and I certainly do not have to try to convince myself that I feel things that I don't.

So, if you are laboring, trying to "create" love, stop.

Just. Fucking. STOP.

Walk away. Never look back. I can't promise that you will find real love somewhere else—but I guarantee it's not going to happen there.

Staying there will certainly destroy your chances of ever finding real love.

Don't thank me
for doing the things
that love should always do.
This is how it's supposed to feel.
Get used to it.

I think we should
make love
and make art
until we don't
see a line
between them
anymore.

THE MIDDLE OF THE road felt like a fault line that night as I walked in slow motion between the rows of police cars and ambulances on either side of me.

Paramedics and police officers zigzagged back and forth, but I walked through them, seemingly unnoticed, as if I were a ghost.

I could feel the entire expanding universe reverse course and begin to collapse around my lungs. Red and blue lights, crackling voices on radios, and the thickest, realest fear I have ever felt, were the only things that existed in that moment.

I made it to within a few feet of her unrecognizable vehicle, upside down in a field, before I was finally noticed by an officer.

He grabbed my arm and guided me away from the scene.

"It doesn't look good. She's not breathing yet."

Everything went black, and I felt the unsympathetic pavement smash into my knees. I gasped for air, but the oxygen that filled my lungs burned with the memory of every breath I ever took before I got the opportunity to breathe the same air as her. Once you've inhaled the kind of air that feels like being alive, the labored breathing of merely surviving will never be enough again.

And I knew: If she didn't start breathing, I was just going to have to stop.

MINE

Loose hair wrapped tightly in relentless fist
It's shocking sometimes the way a neck moves
Darwinian odors hang like a mist
Cries ring out to gods whose ears won't approve

Palm like a stone striking soft flesh echoes
Nostrils flare wide at the sight of red skin
Chipping away at a will that won't let go
Eyes dilated taking in all this sin

An animal knows to go for the throat
All of life flows through the pathways it hides
Something inside needs to feel like death's close
And stand on that line to feel more alive

In all this we know you belong to me
And in that belonging you've been set free

SHE IS MY OXYGEN.

Poets like to say completely meaningless shit like that. But **THIS** fucking bitch...

She is so much more important to me than just oxygen. Not only on really heavy days like today, when my paranoia and anxiety get the best of me, and I truly do not want to be alive...

But *every single day*—when my paranoia and anxiety get the best of me, and I truly do not want to be alive.

She is the reason, every moment of every day, that I make the conscious decision to take the next breaths that continuing to live requires.

No.

She's not my fucking oxygen.

But without her, oxygen wouldn't do me any goddamn good anyway.

On most days,
I don't want to face
the next;
but then I wake
to the sight of your face,
and I think,
"Okay.
I definitely want to do that
one more time."
If I keep living
just "one more time" at a time,
one day I'll be looking back on a long life,
and it will have been a life worth living.

What makes me happy?
When she says ,
"I'm so happy."
That's what makes me happy.

I've always known
that if I was ever
really going to be loved
by anyone,
it was going to take someone
just as fucked up
as I am
to do it.
Now that I've found you,
don't you ever apologize
for being perfect
for me.

Like some kind of beast
I can smell you wanting me
every time I breathe

AND THEN IT HAPPENS.

That insidious little anxious creature that you've held at bay for so long, somewhere in a dark corner of the deepest part of who you are, rises up.

And it grips your throat, and runs jagged claws through the delicate gray matter that occupies your skull.

And for no reason, everything is wrong, and you can't breathe, and the tears flow, and the body shakes.

But I will be there, powerless as I am to do a single thing except hold you.

*But I **will** hold you.*

For a thousand years, if that's how long it takes. Until everything is okay, or as okay as anything every really is for people like you and me.

Because I know that is exactly what you will do for me, when my little red-eyed demons decide, once again, to come out and play.

She told me
she wanted our love
to be an adventure,
but I really wasn't prepared
for the amazing places
she would take me.

What if they only need you
for a little while?
Can you handle that?
Are you strong enough
to be a bridge?

Those we love
often arrive
covered in
figurative
and literal
scars.

Everything in us
wants to erase those scars
and sometimes we let ourselves
believe it can be done.

But love is not a time machine,
and we can't go back
to those dark places they've been
and protect them from the pain
they've already felt.

Those scars they carry
will fade with time,
but they will never disappear.

That's just not how scars work.
The best we can do is love them
in a way that tells them:

*"You're safe now.
No more.
No more scars for you."*

It's okay if they never believe you.
It's okay if you can never make them understand
that you think they are perfect,
and you wouldn't change
a single thing about them.
At least then,
you'll never forget
that you need to keep reminding them.

The amount of time she spends
rolling her eyes at me
might be cause for concern,
were it not for the fact
that I also make sure
she spends a great deal of time
with her eyes rolled back in her skull.

I make myself contemplate
the massive size of the universe we live in,
made up of billions of galaxies,
full of billions of stars,
with billions of planets revolving around them,
across a distance that is damn-near unimaginable.
Somehow this makes the distance between you
    and me
seem just a bit less significant,
and almost bearable.
Almost...

She just feels easy to me.
She's just right,
just as she is.
So when she apologizes
because she thinks she's too much
or too loud
or too complicated
or too difficult
or too messy,
I just want to kick the whole world's ass
for ever making her feel that way.

For most of my life,

no one was down for me.

No one ever had my back.

My corner was always empty.

But when I got off work and I said,

"I need to try to make it to Des Moines

to say goodbye to Grandma,"

she said,

"I'll be ready in five minutes."

Then she drove the first half of the trip,

through the night,

into the teeth of a winter storm,

with the determination of a long-haul trucker.

If you're not sure

what love is supposed to look like,

that's how the fuck you love.

We set our sights so low
where love is concerned.
Often our highest hope
is just to maintain that pheromone-fueled high
of the earliest days of a love story.
But love can grow
so much larger than that.
Love can expand to horizons
you've never dreamt were possible
if you allow it to evolve the way it wants to,
rather than trying to force it to be
whatever you've always been told it should look like.

One day
your dog is going to die,
and I swear to every god
you'll not
dig that hole
alone.

Your Mom
LOVES THIS STORY...

THE STORY OF US

THERE I WAS, in my late thirties, for the second time in about a year, moving back into the room that I learned how to masturbate in.

Earlier, I had briefly moved back into this tiny room in my dad's single-wide trailer after my fourteen-year marriage ended—after I found out about over a decade of the worst kind of betrayal.

With a pretty embarrassing rebound relationship in my rear-view mirror, there I was again. I had taken two days off work to try and frantically make this small room livable for my three daughters and myself on the days that I had them. The hopelessness I felt was almost unbearable, but it had reached a point of stoic acceptance:

I had given up. On life. On love. On everything except getting my daughters raised.

That was my plan. Raise my girls and die—and probably drink a great deal along the way. I was done looking for the love I desperately needed, but just knew could not exist. Not for me, anyway. I was unlovable, I thought, and the acceptance of that fact was almost comforting as I sat on the bunk beds I was putting together and consciously let the need for anyone else's love leave my body.

I knew I wasn't in a good place, but I was process-ing it like a fucking man. And while I had given up on everything being "O.K." I had passed that terri-ble point where I was questioning if I would even survive—and that felt like a victory.

I. Was. *Done*. With. Relationships.

It was the first time I had ever reached that lev-el of jaded, but it still somehow felt comforting. It was then—sitting and thinking, simultaneously giv-ing up and gathering some sort of resolve—that the loud *ping* of a Facebook message shattered the lonely silence.

•••••

Ours is the kind of love story that spends an ex-cruciatingly long time as a tragedy—with both pro-tagonists brought to their absolute fucking break-ing points before anything that resembles a happy ending comes along.

But in hindsight, this was how it was always go-ing to end up. This story was always about **US**. The close calls and missed opportunities were just too perfectly written to have been an accident.

Natasha and I had actually worked together for a brief time in a restaurant when she was seventeen and I was twenty. She was a hostess and I washed dishes—and we never really spoke.

Later, she would come to see a band I was in and hang out with us through mutual friends, but I was already dating the woman who would become my first wife.

Shortly after that, both of us settled into what would be our own personal hells for the next decade and a half or so. Married to people who were unwilling, and ultimately incapable, of loving who we both were. Both our first daughters were born just a few months apart, as were our second daughters. We lived out a parallel desperation, in houses less than five miles apart.

It wasn't until both our second daughters became best friends in kindergarten that our paths crossed again. Birthday parties. Dropping off and picking up little girls for play dates and sleepovers. I was smitten with Natasha, to say the very least, but we never flirted, and we never messaged each other.

She possessed a kind of beauty that seemed to radiate from the inside outward, and I could always tell from her eyes that her life was crushing her just as badly as mine was crushing me. But nothing beyond "How's it going?" and "Have a good day!" was ever spoken between us at the time.

Natasha was, however, the subject of thousands of my most inappropriate thoughts for many years, as we both continued through the motions of trying to save our marriages.

For the children, the old adage goes.

Just as our loveless first marriages had mirrored each other so closely, they both inevitably fell apart around the same time.

But Timing was not yet done being a motherfucker to us, and Natasha was a free woman just a short time before I was a free man.

When I was moving back into my dad's house for the first time, she was already in a relationship with someone else. No one ever knew, and I wouldn't have been able to explain why, but that hurt like hell. I already knew she was The One based on nothing more than a sad look I had seen in her eyes.

Our misfortune continued as I moved in with my first post-divorce relationship: a farm girl with lots of horses and lots more insecurities—and far more jealousy than I was willing to tolerate—and Natasha broke up with hers.

I watched it play out on Facebook and cursed every possible thing that could be cursed for our terrible misfortune. It got worse. Before I came to my senses in the relationship that I was in and loaded all of my things into my car to move back in with my dad, Natasha found someone else

•••••

Ping.

I looked down at my phone and saw her face, and every single bit of resolve I had built up to never EVER be in a relationship again disappeared instantly. Her face is the only face that could have done that to me.

"Well, okay. I guess I'm going to marry this bitch," I said out loud before I even opened the message to read it.

Probably not the most romantic way to start a relationship, but that is exactly where it began—she just didn't know it yet.

The fact that her profile picture was her and another man, with the word "love" superimposed over it, meant exactly not-a-goddamn-thing to me. It was time to end this shit—or *begin it,* rather. The missed opportunities would stop right there. No more liking each other's Facebook posts and knowing we had *EVERYTHING* in common without doing something about it.

I didn't really give a shit what her message said when I opened it; she was going to know how I felt about her on that day.

"Hey...not meaning to be nosy, but did you and your girl split up? Hope you're doing well! I love seeing your pictures of the girls :) they always look like they are having the best time with you!"

That's all it said. Harmless enough, really, and she insists to this very day that she wasn't trying to make a move. But it was enough of a move to ensure that I made mine.

Still, though, she was with someone else, and I'm really not that kind of asshole, so I played it like the gentleman that I truly am. I told her that the woman I had been with had actually gotten to the point that she was even jealous of the time I spent with my daughters, and that was a line that nobody was going to cross with me, so I was back at my dad's.

We talked back and forth for a bit and then she mentioned something that made me think perhaps things weren't going as well for her and her man as her Facebook profile picture seemed to indicate.

"But you're doing good now, right?"

It turned out, things were not good at all. He needed his "space"–and that's all I needed to hear. With a combination of lovestruck, teenage nervousness and the resolve of a grown ass man with absolutely nothing to lose, I began to type:

"I'm gonna have to be honest here. I'm not sure I can give you fair advice in this situation without it being biased. I've thought you were an amazing person since before either one of us was divorced. When [redacted ex-wife] and I split, I really wanted to talk to you, but then you were with [redacted ex-boyfriend]. You have no idea how stupid I felt when you two split, and I was already with someone else. Now I'm single again, and you're not.

But since you contacted me, I guess I don't feel like a creep for telling you this now. That being said, I'm still probably capable of giving legit relationship advice without letting my own feelings get in the way, but it wouldn't be fair for me to do that without you knowing how I felt. So if you really think it's worth fighting for, then fight your ass off and see what happens.

"That's the advice I would give anyone else right now. I'm definitely not rooting against you guys. I'm too grown up for that. But if it doesn't work out, just remember what I've said, and maybe we could get to know each other, slowly, and see what happens. Hopefully you don't think

I'm an asshole for all of that, but I would feel like more of an asshole not saying it."

It felt like every bit of wanting her that I had experienced over the past several years was crammed into the next thirty-four excruciating minutes as I waited for her reply. But I wasn't nervous. It was as if every bit of pain I had been through in my life had prepared me for this. Just to put myself out there, and to be perfectly fine with whatever came of it. I was equally ready to accept rejection—and also somehow firmly convinced that that was not going to happen.

This was my story, and I knew it, as if I were watching it unfold in the third person. I had been forged into the perfect combination of hopeless romantic and completely fucking unbreakable. Finally ready to spread my ribcage and expose what was inside, with no fear of what might happen when I did.

I also knew that I wasn't just prepared to survive—I had become what I was specifically for this woman. That part makes no sense, given that I really only knew that Natasha was hotter than fifteen motherfuckers, and she had great taste in music. But I was absolutely certain that she was my reason to be here. I had seen it in her eyes, standing on my front porch, dropping her daughter off to spend the night–years before that fateful day. A knowledge beyond words–and it all made sense to me in that moment.

Her message started with:

"Wow...I definitely wasn't expecting that!"

and ended with:

"I've honestly had the same thoughts about you, but probably wouldn't have said anything if you hadn't, though."

In between were a lot more details about just how bad her situation really was, and how she was planning on moving back to her house after that upcoming weekend. That made me feel a little less like a douchebag, but honestly, I would have clubbed a thousand baby seals to be with this woman and felt absolutely no remorse.

We spent the next several days texting without even getting to see each other. I was working third shift, and she would stay up almost all night, and we would talk until she finally stopped returning my texts for the evening, when I knew she had fallen asleep.

The intensity of those days was exhilarating. It was like we were having a competition to see which of us could scare the other one off first. We were both in the exact same place. We really wanted this, and we definitely didn't want to give up on love altogether. But we were sure as shit going to be loved for exactly who we really were, if we were going to be loved at all.

So we told each other every single thing that everyone else had ever hated about us, and we fell in love with all of those things in each other. It was as if we were seeing each other naked, and we still hadn't even laid eyes on each other since this whole thing had started.

On the fourth day of our whirlwind courtship, I was working a twelve-hour shift, and we arranged to meet at Cracker Barrel the next morning when I got off. I was ecstatic to finally look at Natasha face to face for the first time since I had told her how I felt about her, but as the end of my shift approached, I realized what a dreadful mistake I had made by agreeing to meet her after I had been up all night.

When I was working thirds, my body—and, more importantly, my brain—would completely shut down at the end of the shift, and the only safe place for me to be was in a bed. I was still far too excited to see her to back out, so I met her as soon as I got off work.

Needless to say, I was a complete fucking mess, and I can't believe she didn't run away right then, never to look back. I remember running my mouth way too much, and giggling. I giggled my way through that awkward breakfast, like a little girl on mushrooms.

When we left, I walked her to her car, and somehow was able to stop my ridiculous giggling long enough to get serious. I held her face in both hands, and for the first time, I really looked into her eyes.

"This is the part where everything is going to be okay for both of us, Natasha," I said. "You're going to be okay. I'm going to be okay. We're going to be okay together."

Then I kissed her, and everything in my world felt like a fairy tale. A fairy tale with two very damaged grown people, and one that wasn't quite ready to really begin just yet.

●●●●●

What transpired over the next few days was not pleasant, but I believe it was absolutely necessary for both Natasha and me to learn the things about ourselves—and each other—that we really needed to know to move forward with this.

Whereas I had survived a long, miserable marriage and one post-marriage relationship with just the wrong person, Natasha had been through the same kind of dead marriage, followed by *two* terrible relationships where she was mentally and physically abused, and at times had members of her own family turned against her.

Life had chewed her up and spit her right back out into my lap. She was literally still trying to get all of her things moved back to her own home, amid the intensity of everything her and I were sharing, and I think she may have broken under the pressure a little bit. And that was completely understandable, but painful as fuck nevertheless.

One moment, we were messaging each other, sharing our souls, and planning. The next, she was losing her mind and texting me at work while she was driving around, in no condition to be doing so.

I told her she needed to get her ass home, then I left work and went to her house to make sure she was there, just so I could be sure she was safe. She

wasn't in a good place. I think the weight of everything she had been through came crashing down
on her all at once, and she was broken and terrified
by it.

I told her she needed to take some time to process all of that, and all of *this*, and she could get
back to me when—or if—she wanted to.

Over the next three days, I learned a great deal
about myself. About the progress I had made as a
man, and as a human. I gave Natasha the time I had
told her I would give her, and I didn't try to contact
her. But I wasn't playing some childish game either.
I had no strategy. I was just going to do what I said
I would do. By this time, I was absolutely invested
as fuck in this woman. You can think what you will
of me, but I was in love with her from that very first
day, if not before.

Now I had to make myself let go. Not in a frustrat-
ed or angry or even a sad way. Just in a *grown man*
way, where I understood how damaged she was.
And as much as I was ready for her, I realized that
maybe she just wasn't ready for me.

Timing never had been kind to our story, but I
had seen a chance, and I had taken it. And maybe
that still wasn't going to be enough. And that was
okay, too.

I won't say I didn't shed a few tears, but I also had something that felt a lot like faith telling me to chill the fuck out, because everything was going to be okay.

I had been doing a little writing, and posting it on my Facebook, and on Day 3, I wrote a poem about where I was at that point and shared it:

You know what's going to happen
And you know it's going to hurt like hell
And when it's over
Another piece of you will be gone
And you'll cry into a pillow
And move on
But you do it anyway
Because someone else needs you to
And you put their needs
Before your own instincts
Because you are human
And you're pretty fucking good at it...

She finally texted me:

"I feel like everything you've been posting is about me..."

259

I couldn't deny she was correct. I may have promised to leave her alone, but that didn't stop me from throwing my thinly-veiled feelings on the Internet.

I told her that I just wanted to get the chance to hold her face again, and tell her that she was going to be okay, and I was going to be okay, and we were both going to be okay—*together*.

She asked me if we could meet up the next evening, and of course I agreed. My oldest daughter, who was also my closest confidant, and the only one who knew about all of this, insisted on dressing me. She had guessed I was talking about Natasha when I mentioned I was talking to someone.

"I always thought you two should be together," she had said.

Natasha and I met at a park and drank some cheap wine. The conversation was slow and serious, but she was ready now, and we both knew it.

We went to a bar, and everything seemed more relaxed at that point. She was okay. I was okay. *WE* were okay.

And we were just beginning to feel how wonderful being okay could really feel.

•••••

We left the bar together that night and went back to her place and...

...and that's probably where I'm going to conclude this story.

At the end of all of the hell we had both been through, and the beginning of the best thing that has ever happened to either one of us.

For all of our big talk in those earliest days about "taking it slow," we were married four months later.

And I promise all of you: I have fallen more in love with this incredible woman every single day that we have been together.

She was my
Knight in shining armor.

Carl Sagan
taught me how vast
the universe is.

And I'd traverse
every goddamn bit of it
just to get to—

YOU.

If you or someone you know is suicidal or in emotional distress, contact the

National Suicide Prevention Lifeline

1-800-273-TALK (8255)

or chat live online at
www.suicidepreventionlifeline.org

Trained crisis workers are available to talk 24 hours a day, 7 days a week.

Your confidential and toll-free call goes to the nearest crisis center in the Lifeline national network.

These centers provide crisis counseling and mental health referrals.

Turn the page for a special
preview of

The collection that
started it all!

Available from
Big Small Town Books!

We can be monsters
You and I
Just like everyone else
But without the disguise

It could never be enough
I will never be done
There will be no moment
When my lips have had their fill of yours
It is the kind of thirst
That can never possibly be quenched
Always
Every moment
My entire soul screams
Just
One
More

On Sunday
We worship
Each other

We were both too exhausted

From long roads

To hide who we really were any longer

We were both too weary

From long years

To try to be anything other than ourselves

We had no strength

For effort

Left

Then we found each other

And we were home

And it was easy

And now…

We can rest

There's just something about
The way she stands
Her posture
Shoulders back
Chin up
Back arched
So fucking sexy
I've not looked at her one single time
Without my mind instantly fantasizing
About all the unholy things I want to do with her
    naked body...
But it's so much more than just
Intoxicating primal lust
When she stands like that
I really believe she might just take over the world
The whole fucking world
And when she does
I want to be right there beside her

No man

Has ever needed

Supervision

As much as I do

And no woman

Has ever made

Being supervised

Feel as much like freedom

As she does

You know that warm feeling
In your gut
That makes you hard
And makes you wet?
You think that's love
Don't you?
That's not love
That's just biology's way
Of making biological shit
Seem a lot more fun
Love is even more primal than that
It is a moment-to-moment
Fight-or-flight decision
Love is found in those moments
When the hair on your neck stands up
And you bare your teeth
And protect each other's necks
Love is when you know that
Good or bad
Day or night
Win or lose
Live or die...
This is your fucking person
And you're going to face everything
Together

It was just a moment
Both of us on our way
From different point As
To different point Bs
Just a moment
With you in my arms
And your lips pressed to mine
And it made the entire day
Beautiful

Let's just be
Damaged
Together

I don't call her
"Darling"
When I write about her
Because in real life I say
"I love you, bitch"
And she says
"I love you, motherfucker"
And we both get those
Silly little butterflies in our stomach
That's the kind of love
I've always wanted

It never feels
Freaky or filthy
When we do all those
Wonderful things
We do to each other
It just feels like
Making love

It's almost as if
The moment we found each other
Some sort of Karmic balance
Was thrown violently off its axis
And ever since that instant
Not one single thing
Has gone right for us
That's okay
The universe can do
Whatever it needs to do
To reset its equilibrium
And when the dust settles
We'll be standing right here together
Exhausted from laughter
And amazing sex
With four middle fingers in the air

Poets write
Intense lines like
"I would die for you"
And then that passion
Unbacked by resolve
Disappears
As soon as the ink runs out
But you and I both know
I'm not really a poet

Being loved by you
Makes every breath
Feel less like a chore
And more
Like a miracle

She still has these
Little moments of anxiety
When she thinks
She doesn't "deserve" me
And she's scared she might lose me
She doesn't understand
That I was never a man worth having
Until she gave me the freedom
To be myself
And there is no fucking way
That I will ever let that go

And I still
Wake up
Wanting
You

If it takes more than just one lifetime

And more words than I can write

If it takes more hugs than my arms can handle

And more kisses than my lips can take

If we have to make love even more than

My insatiable appetite can fathom

I will make her understand

How deep

And unconditional

My love for her really is

And more importantly

She will know that she deserves

Far more than that

And that I am the one

Who won the lottery

When we found each other

Photo Credit: Natasha Welch

J. WARREN WELCH is a husband, father of daughters, lover of squats and deadlifts, wearer of leggings, commenter on social issues, podcast host, and writer of prose and poetry who resides in East Tennessee.

You can find him on social media at:

 @j.warren.welch

 J. Warren Welch

 @J_Warren_Welch